W9-BAJ-260

SUPER BOWL SUPERSTARS

SANTONIO HOLMES
and the
Pittsburgh Steelers

SUPER BOWL XLIII

by Michael Sandler

Consultant: Norries Wilson
Head Football Coach
Columbia University

BEARPORT
PUBLISHING

New York, New York

Credits

Cover and Title Page, © Len Redkoles/Getty Images; 4, © Chris McGrath/Getty Images; 5, © Win McNamee/Getty Images; 7, © Damon Higgins/The Palm Beach Post/ZUMA Press; 8, © Bill Ward/Tampa Tribune; 9, © David Spencer/Palm Beach Post/ZUMA Press; 10, © Bob DeMay/Akron Beacon Journal/KRT/Newscom; 11, © AP Images/Gene J. Puskar; 12, © Michael Fabus/Getty Images; 13, © Christopher A. Record/Charlotte Observer/MCT/Newscom; 14, © Andy Lyons/Getty Images; 15, © Chris Graythen/Getty Images; 16, © Rob Tringali/Sportschrome/Getty Images; 17, © Mark Cornelison/Lexington Herald-Leader/MCT/Landov; 18, © Brian Blanco/Bradenton Herald/MCT/Landov; 19, © Rob Hobson/UPI/Landov; 20, © John Angelillo/UPI/Landov; 21, © Reuters/Pierre Ducharme/Landov; 22L, © AP Images/Mark Duncan; 22R, © zsports/Newscom; 22 Background, © Terry Gilliam/MCT/Landau.

Publisher: Kenn Goin
Senior Editor: Lisa Wiseman
Creative Director: Spencer Brinker
Design: Debrah Kaiser
Photo Researcher: Picture Perfect Professionals, LLC

Library of Congress Cataloging-in-Publication Data

Sandler, Michael, 1965–
 Santonio Holmes and the Pittsburgh Steelers : Super Bowl XLIII / by Michael Sandler; consultant, Norries Wilson.
     p. cm. (Super Bowl superstars)
 Includes bibliographical references and index.
 ISBN-13: 978-1-59716-968-4 (library binding)
 ISBN-10: 1-59716-968-4 (library binding)
 1. Holmes, Santonio. 2. Football players—United States—Biography. 3. Pittsburgh Steelers (Football team) 4. Super Bowl (43rd : 2009 : Tampa, Fla.) I. Wilson, Norries. II. Title.
 GV939.H57S36 2010
 796.332092—dc22
 (B)

                                     2009015491

For more information, write to Bearport Publishing Company, Inc., 101 Fifth Avenue, Suite 6R, New York, New York 10003. Printed in the United States of America.

10 9 8 7 6 5 4 3 2 1

☆ Contents ☆

Meeting the Challenge

Super Bowl XLIII (43) was coming down to the wire. Both teams were fighting to the very end, refusing to lose.

The Pittsburgh Steelers had started the game strong. Then the Arizona Cardinals roared back, taking the lead with just two minutes left to play.

Now the Steelers were beginning their final **drive** of the season. They needed to make big plays. If they didn't, they'd lose. Which player would step up to the challenge?

"I'm the guy," said Santonio Holmes to quarterback Ben Roethlisberger. Could the young **wide receiver** back up his words?

Ben Roethlisberger (right) talks with Santonio Holmes (left) during Super Bowl XLIII (43).

Santonio reacts after a play during Super Bowl XLIII (43) in 2009.

Super Bowl XLIII (43) had special meaning for both teams. The Arizona Cardinals were trying to win their first championship. At the same time, the Pittsburgh Steelers were trying to become the first NFL team to win six Super Bowls.

A Tough Life

Santonio Holmes was used to tough situations. He grew up in Belle Glade, Florida. In his rough-and-tumble neighborhood, there were no factories, big stores, or even movie theaters. Most people couldn't find jobs. Santonio's mother, Patricia Brown, was lucky to have one.

Every morning, this single mom woke up at 3 A.M. and caught a bus out to a farm. Working all day packing corn into boxes, she barely made enough money to support her four sons.

With his mother working long hours, Santonio was left at home to take care of his three younger brothers. In the morning, he got them ready for school. In the afternoon, he watched them until his mother got home from work.

To earn extra money for clothing and shoes, Santonio chased rabbits in the sugarcane fields outside of Belle Glade. He could sell each rabbit he caught for three dollars.

Santonio's mother, Patricia, with one of his brothers

Three-Sport Star

To catch rabbits, a person needs to move fast, and Santonio had plenty of speed. His quickness made him a natural in three sports—basketball, track, and football.

At Glades Central High School, Santonio's basketball team was one of Florida's best. His **4 x 400 meter relay** team won two state track titles. Not surprisingly, his football team was also a winner. Santonio was the star wide receiver and, by senior year, one of the state's top pass catchers.

Even though he spent a lot of time playing sports, Santonio never slacked off on his schoolwork. In 2002, he graduated from Glades Central with a 3.4 **GPA**.

Santonio (far left) and some of his track teammates

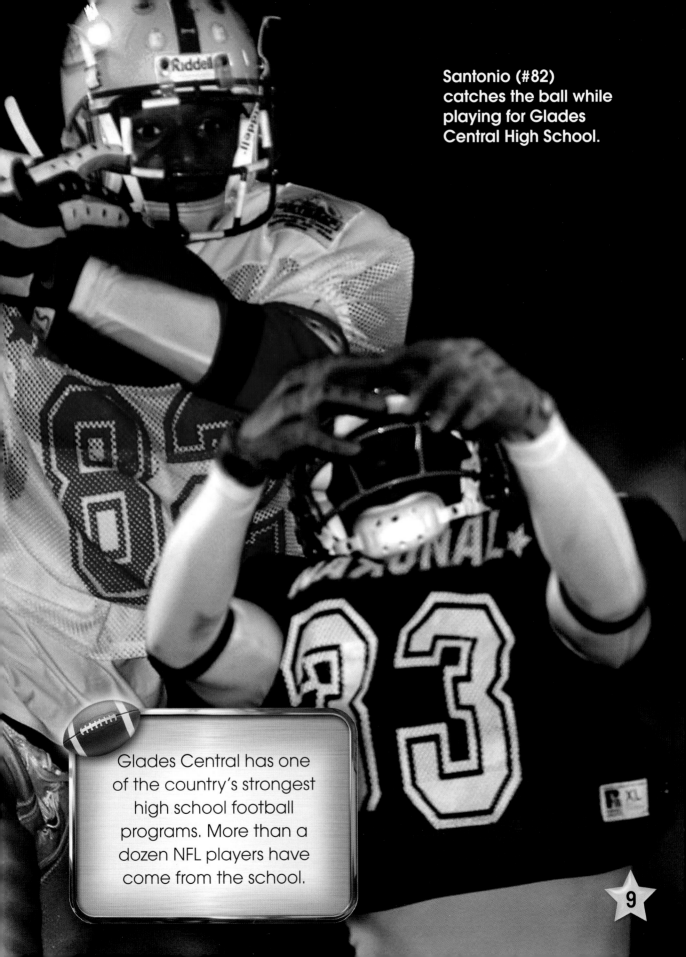

Santonio (#82) catches the ball while playing for Glades Central High School.

Glades Central has one of the country's strongest high school football programs. More than a dozen NFL players have come from the school.

On to Ohio State

Santonio went on to college at Ohio State University. He chose the school because of its strong football team—especially its **offense**. Ohio State's coach liked his team to pass, so wide receivers like Santonio saw plenty of action.

In high school, Santonio had worked hard. His coach called him a "first-to-practice, last-to-leave kid." At Ohio State, he didn't change his hard-working ways. One summer, rather than spending his vacation at home in Florida, he stayed in Ohio to work on his **conditioning**.

Santonio's hard work paid off in April 2006. The Pittsburgh Steelers chose him in the NFL **draft**'s first round.

In three seasons at Ohio State, Santonio (#4) caught 243 passes for 2,295 yards (2,099 m) and 25 touchdowns.

Eager to help his family by earning an NFL paycheck, Santonio left college one year early to play for the Pittsburgh Steelers. Here he is on draft day.

After Santonio signed his contract with the Steelers, he bought a house for his mom and stepfather. "They've been working for the past 30 years," he said. "Now it's my turn to help them."

Playing for Pittsburgh

Santonio was joining his favorite team and one of the NFL's best. The Steelers had won five championships, including Super Bowl XL (40) in February 2006.

The team already had great wide receivers, including Super Bowl **MVP** Hines Ward. Still, Santonio quickly showed he had the skills to contribute. Midway through his **rookie** year in 2006, he broke into the starting lineup. He finished the season with 49 **receptions**. Then in 2007, Santonio led the Steelers in both receptions and touchdowns.

Santonio (#10) runs the ball down the field in a 2007 game against the New York Jets.

Santonio didn't just play wide receiver for Pittsburgh. He also returned **punts**.

Santonio returned a punt 65 yards (59 m) for a touchdown against the Carolina Panthers during his rookie season.

13

The 2008-2009 Steelers

In 2008, the Steelers were a terrific team. Coach Mike Tomlin had them playing great football at both ends of the field. On **defense**, **linebacker** James Harrison **anchored** a group that gave up fewer yards than any other team in the league that season. On offense, **Pro Bowl** quarterback Ben Roethlisberger guided the way, often throwing passes to Santonio and Hines Ward.

The Steelers finished 12-4 and won the **AFC North** title. Then they scored playoff wins over the San Diego Chargers and the Baltimore Ravens. Next up was Super Bowl XLIII (43) against the Arizona Cardinals.

In 2008, James Harrison (#92) was voted NFL Defensive Player of the Year. Here he is sacking Ryan Fitzpatrick (#11) of the Cincinnati Bengals.

Santonio's 67-yard (61-m) punt return touchdown helped the Steelers to a playoff win over San Diego.

The Super Bowl

The Cardinals were the Super Bowl's surprise team. Arizona barely made it into the playoffs, but once they were there, they won three straight games with the help of **veteran** quarterback Kurt Warner.

When Super Bowl XLIII (43) began, the Steelers burst into the lead with a field goal. A touchdown by running back Gary Russell extended Pittsburgh's lead. Then James Harrison **intercepted** a Kurt Warner pass in the **end zone**. He ran it all the way back for a 100-yard (91-m) touchdown.

The confident Steelers went into the fourth quarter with a 20-7 lead. Kurt Warner, however, was about to strike back.

Cardinals quarterback Kurt Warner had previously won a Super Bowl with the St. Louis Rams.

James Harrison (#92) runs for a 100-yard (91-m) touchdown interception.

Harrison's 100-yard (91-m) interception return was the longest play of any kind in Super Bowl history!

Losing the Lead

First, Kurt found star receiver Larry Fitzgerald four times on an 87-yard (80-m) touchdown drive. Pittsburgh's lead shrank to 20-14. A penalty cut the lead even more. The score was now 20-16.

Then Kurt and Larry struck again on a 64-yard (59-m) touchdown play. With just 2 minutes and 37 seconds left in the game, the Cardinals were ahead, 23-20! The Steelers were in trouble.

Pittsburgh had time for one last drive, however. Santonio begged Ben to use him. The Steelers' quarterback agreed. Twice he threw quick, short passes to Santonio. Then Ben launched a bomb—a 40-yard (37-m) pass that Santonio caught right at the 6-yard (5-m) line.

Larry Fitzgerald (#11) races down the field.

On Pittsburgh's final drive of Super Bowl XLIII (43), Santonio gained 73 of the Steelers' 78 total yards (67 of the total 71 m).

Super Santonio

Now close enough to score, Ben looked for Santonio one last time. The speedy wide receiver ran to the corner of the end zone. He stretched out as far as he could in front of three Arizona defenders. Somehow, leaning on his tiptoes, he grabbed Ben's pass before tumbling out of bounds.

Pittsburgh fans held their breath. Officials checked the replay. Had Santonio kept his feet **inbounds** while making the catch? Yes! The officials signaled touchdown. Pittsburgh had the lead.

The game ended 35 seconds later with a **fumble** by Kurt Warner. Santonio and the Steelers were champions.

"I knew it was a touchdown, 100 percent," said Santonio.

A receiver must have both feet completely inbounds when he catches the ball. If he doesn't, the pass is ruled **incomplete**.

Santonio was named MVP of Super Bowl XLIII (#43). Here he is with his trophy.

There were other key players on the Pittsburgh Steelers who helped win Super Bowl XLIII (43). Here are two of them.

⭐ Ben Roethlisberger #7

Position: Quarterback
Born: 3/2/1982 in Lima, Ohio
Height: 6' 5" (1.96 m)
Weight: 241 pounds (109 kg)
Key Plays: Completed 21 of 30 passes for 256 yards (234 m); threw the game-winning touchdown pass to Santonio Holmes with less than one minute remaining in the game.

⭐ James Harrison #92

Position: Linebacker
Born: 5/4/1978 in Akron, Ohio
Height: 6' 0" (1.83 m)
Weight: 242 pounds (110 kg)
Key Play: Intercepted a Kurt Warner pass and returned it 100 yards (91 m) for a touchdown

Glossary

AFC North (AY-EFF-SEE NORTH) a four-team group in the American Football Conference

anchored (ANG-kurd) played a key role; supported

conditioning (kuhn-DISH-uh-ning) working out to stay in shape

defense (di-FENSS) the part of a team that has the job of stopping the other team from scoring

draft (DRAFT) an event in which professional teams take turns choosing college players to play for them

drive (DRIVE) a series of plays in which the team with the ball tries to move down the field

end zone (END ZOHN) the area at either end of a football field where touchdowns are scored

4 x 400 meter relay (FOR BYE for-HUHN-druhd MEE-tur REE-lay) a track relay race in which four team members each run 400 meters (437 yards)

fumble (FUM-buhl) a ball that is dropped by the player who has it

GPA (JEE-PEE-AY) grade point average; 3.4 means the student has a high B average

inbounds (IN-boundz) inside the lines that mark the edge of a field

incomplete (in-kuhm-PLEET) not caught according to the rules; not counting

intercepted (in-tur-SEPT-id) caught a pass meant for a player on the other team

linebacker (LINE-bak-ur) a defensive player who lines up behind the first line of defensive players

MVP (EM-VEE-PEE) most valuable player

offense (AW-fenss) the part of a team that has the job of scoring

Pro Bowl (PROH BOHL) the yearly All-Star game for the season's best NFL players

punts (PUHNTS) plays in which one team kicks the ball downfield to give possession to the other team

receptions (ri-SEP-shuhnz) passes that are caught

rookie (RUK-ee) first year in the league

veteran (VET-ur-uhn) a player with a lot of experience

wide receiver (WIDE ri-SEE-vur) a player whose job it is to catch passes

Bibliography

Acee, Kevin. "Steelers' Holmes Traces Speed to Humble, Rabbit-Chasing Roots." *San Diego Union Tribune* (January 30, 2009).

Darlington, Jeff. "Pittsburgh Steelers' Santonio Holmes Makes the Right Choices." *Miami Herald* (January 13, 2009).

Dulac, Gerry. "Closeup: The No. 1 Pick, Santonio Holmes." *The Pittsburgh Post-Gazette* (April 30, 2006).

NFL.com

Read More

Macrae, Sloan. *The Pittsburgh Steelers (America's Greatest Teams).* New York: PowerKids Press (2009).

Sandler, Michael. *Ben Roethlisberger.* New York: Bearport (2009).

Sandler, Michael. *Hines Ward and the Pittsburgh Steelers: Super Bowl XL.* New York: Bearport (2007).

Learn More Online

To learn more about Santonio Holmes, the Pittsburgh Steelers, and the Super Bowl, visit **www.bearportpublishing.com/SuperBowlSuperstars**

Index